ROADS Publishing
149 Lower Baggot Street
Dublin 2
Ireland

www.roads.co

First published 2017

1

Lisbon: The Considered Guide

Text copyright
© ROADS Publishing

Design and layout copyright
© ROADS Publishing

Photographs
© The copyright holders, pg. 142

Cover image
© Barbara Staubach/ARTUR IMAGES

All of the businesses herein were chosen at the discretion of the publishers.
No payments or incentives were offered or received to ensure inclusion.

Art direction by
Alessio Avventuroso

Designed by
Agenzia del Contemporaneo

Printed in Italy
Grafiche Damiani – Faenza Group SpA

978-1-909399-94-5

Lisbon

The Considered Guide

Growing up, travel was a major part of my life. It was and remains an integral source of education and inspiration. When I travel, I actively search out the most interesting and innovative places. As a rule, I ask my friends and contacts in each city for a list of their favourite places. I then keep and share with others my lists of places both recommended and those I discovered myself. Therefore, I decided to create the kind of travel guide that I myself would find useful: a carefully edited selection of the best places in a city – a book that is practical, beautiful, and, crucially, trustworthy.

The Considered Guide reflects the desires of the discerning traveller who cares deeply about how they spend their valuable time and money, and who appreciates impeccable service, beautiful design and attention to detail at every price level.

I am proud to say that I visited each and every place in this guide, and can vouch for the quality of each of them as personal recommendations.

Danielle Ryan
Founder of ROADS

Introduction

With its terracotta rooftops and coastal setting, the picturesque city of Lisbon is currently having something of a moment. It's warm throughout the year, but never too hot, and very easy to get around, making it a popular spot for a city break, but thankfully not overrun by tourists.

The Portuguese capital is one of the oldest cities in the world, and the oldest in Western Europe. On arrival, you will get a sense of this long history from the crumbling mansions and walls of beautiful tiles that line the hilly streets. Within its Moorish and medieval quarters, however, you will quickly see evidence of the forward-looking and dynamic character of the city, with chic bars, designer ateliers and concept stores on every corner. This blend of old and new will be reinforced as you sip cocktails on a trendy terrace bar and hear fado – a Portuguese style of singing from the early nineteenth century – coming from a nearby taberna.

Of the many peaks and troughs of Lisbon's long history, it was at its most dominant during the Age of Discovery, and glorious remnants of this once-powerful maritime empire are in evidence throughout. From the late fifteenth century, it was home to the world's greatest explorers – Vasco da Gama, Magellan and Prince Henry the Navigator – and the point of departure of many significant voyages. During the sixteenth century, Lisbon was the capital of an empire that spread from South America to Asia, and the European hub for the trade of spices, sugar, and textiles.

Another piece of history strongly in evidence here is the catastrophic earthquake of 1755. Its impact almost completely destroyed the city, and knocked most of Lisbon's palaces and libraries to the ground. The 1st Marquis of Pombal, who held the position akin to Prime Minister at the time, set about rebuilding the city. This gave rise to what is known as 'Pombaline' architecture, which is particularly prominent in downtown Lisbon and is characterised by a restrained neoclassical style and the use of the azulejo tiling. The buildings are generally four storeys high with an arcade on the lower floor, as seen in the Praça do Comércio. Interestingly, they were amongst the first anti-seismic structures ever built.

These days, Lisbon is a thriving, ambitious city. This new exuberance began, one could argue, when the city was the European Capital of Culture in 1994, and gathered pace with the hosting of Expo 1998 – for which Parque das Nações was constructed – marking the 500th anniversary of Vasco da Gama's discovery of a sea route to India. The new prosperity Lisbon has subsequently enjoyed has brought with it many social and cultural changes to the very fabric of the city, with previously derelict areas brimming with edgy new start-ups, boutique hotels and shops

Lisbon is set on seven hills overlooking the Atlantic Ocean. Combining its geographical position with the imposing São Jorge Castle and the scattered white-domed cathedrals, the city offers its visitors some extraordinary views, which explains the prevalence of rooftop bars and terraces. Another one of the many features that makes Lisbon a joy for its visitors is the fact that each of the bairros (neighbourhoods) has its own distinct character. This means that while you feel like you are in a bustling European capital, you can equally enjoy a much more intimate experience in the various areas of the city, from the Moorish labyrinthine streets of Alfama, to the imperial waterfront of Belém, to the raucousness of Bairro Alto.

Lisboetas (natives of Lisbon) are friendly, cosmopolitan people who are welcoming to visitors and open to having a good time. It's a stylish and artistic city, with much to offer the imagination. Visitors these days remark that there is a buzz around the streets that is difficult to define, but you can be assured that you will return feeling energised and inspired.

There is no doubt that the labyrinthine streets of central Lisbon are best explored on foot, but happily there are numerous efficient and inexpensive options for over- and underground public transport to help you get around quickly and to alleviate the burden of the steepest climbs. Buses and metro trains are frequent and dependable, and although not always the quickest way around, the iconic Lisbon trams and funiculars are charming flourishes for a visit. There are a number of options for day and multiple-journey passes, including the new Travelling all Lisboa card (€10 for 24 hours) and the Lisboa Card (€18.50/€31.50/€39 for 1/2/3 days), which, alongside unlimited travel, gives free or discounted entry to dozens of attractions. The Citymapper mobile app (citymapper.com/lisboa) is a good way to access up-to-the-minute transport information.

Getting around

From the airport
aerobus.pt

Lisbon's Portela Airport is just 7km north of the city. The Aerobus leaves every 20 minutes from 7.40am to 8.15pm and is the most cost-effective choice (tickets €3.35 from the driver). Regular city buses are cheaper, but involve more circuitous routes. Taxis are available 24 hours, and you should expect to pay €15-20 to the city centre. This does not include supplements for luggage or non-standard hours (late nights, weekends) so be vigilant about overcharging. A prepaid voucher is a great option; these can be purchased in Arrivals.

Taxis

City taxis are good value compared to other cities, but prices do go up after 9pm, on weekends and on public holidays. These can be hailed on the street (look out for the green light). Central journeys are unlikely to cost more than €10.

Metro
metrolisboa.pt

The four-line metro is fast, cheap and clean. Fares begin at €1.45 for one journey in one zone. Unlike some other multi-journey passes, the Travelling all Lisboa card includes the metro. Lines operate between 6.30am and 1am.

Buses and Trams
carris.pt

Carris operates the bus and tram systems in Lisbon. Bus services run from as early as 5am until as late as 11pm (check the website for timetables); tickets start at €1.80, but buying a multi-journey or unlimited ticket is recommended. The tram network is small but iconic. A trip on the famed Tram 28 is a crowded but fun way to get your bearings.

Elevators
carris.transportlisboa.pt

Lisbon's four elevators (three funiculars and one lift) were declared national monuments in 2002. These century-old elevators give convenient access to some of the trickier-to-access city sights. They comprise the Elevador de Santa Justa (Largo do Carmo to Rua do Ouro), Ascensor da Glória (Praça dos Restauradores to Bairro Alto), Ascensor da Bica (Rua da São Paulo to Largo do Calhariz), and Elevador do Lavra (Largo da Anunciada

to Travessa Forno do Torel). Access is free with many day tickets and tourist cards.

Trains
cp.pt

If the length of your stay allows a trip out of the city centre, the train is extremely good value and a pleasant way to travel. The journey to the seaside village of Cascais is especially scenic, and costs approximately €5 return. Huge crowds flock here during summer months, but trains are frequent.

Hotels

Bairro Alto Hotel

The beloved Bairro Alto Hotel is located in the heart of it all, between the bohemian Bairro Alto neighbourhood and the trendy Chiado area. Comprising fifty-five bedrooms and a well-equipped wellness centre, the confident airy interior, housed behind the late eighteenth-century façade, is notable for the elegant juxtaposition of period and contemporary features. Flores Restaurant, on the ground floor, provides an elegant dining experience with gourmet tapas among the fare on offer, but the jewel in the crown is the romantic rooftop terrace bar, Terraço BA, from which you can take in fantastic views of the Tagus River. It really has everything you need in a small hotel.

€€€

—

Praça Luis de Camões 2, 1200-243 Lisboa
bairroaltohotel.com
+351 21 340 82 88

The Independente

Could this be the coolest hostel ever? Facing the Miradouro de São Pedro de Alcântara, and with all the grandeur you would expect from the former official residence of the Swiss ambassador, the Independente puts an effortlessly cool twist on the building's high ceilings, parquet floors and shuttered windows. Equally hip are the two popular on-site restaurants: Decandente (see pg. 66), serving modern Portuguese food with an emphasis on local ingredients, and the rooftop fusion restaurant Insólito (see pg. 67), which boasts great views of the old town. Guests can choose between the three-tiered bunk beds of the minimal-chic dorm rooms or avail of one of the four suites on the top floor for a more private experience. Breakfast is served on the rooftop.

€

Rua de São Pedro de Alcântara 81, 1250-238 Lisboa
theindependente.pt
+351 21 346 1381

The Lisbonaire Apartments

With prices starting at €35 per person, these nineteen contemporary apartments are stylish, clean and welcoming. Ideally located near the Glória funicular and a short stroll from the Bairro Alto area, the otherwise minimalist apartments are adorned by inscriptions, tags, and illustrations, each by a different local designer, taking inspiration from the visual language of the local area. Each of the apartments is air-conditioned and well equipped with exclusively locally produced furniture and all the essentials for a short stay. The complex also boasts a fitness centre, a communal lounge, a kids' playroom, a pool table, and a rooftop terrace.

€

—

Rua da Glória 16, 1250-116 Lisboa
lisbonaire.com
+351 912 769 797

Memmo Alfama

Nestled in the busy twisting streets of the city's old
Alfama quarter is Memmo Alfama, whose forty-two
bedrooms are incongruously clean and minimal, with
white walls, crisp linens and shuttered windows.
According to architect Samuel Torres de Carvalho,
the design aims to create the feeling of 'a big cosy
home'. As you arrive, you'll be greeted by a mural by
renowned conceptual artist Vhils and a warm living
space functions as the check-in area. Enjoy the red-
tiled rooftop pool and take in the glorious view of the
Tagus Estaury from the vast terrace as you sample the
local wine. Adults only.

€€

—

Travessa das Merceeiras 27, 1100-348 Lisboa
memmohotels.com
+351 210 495 660

Palácio Belmonte

Tucked away off a cobbled street, in the battlements of the Castelo de São Jorge, sits one of Lisbon's most opulent residences. Built in 1449, it was once the home of one of Portugal's most famous adventurers, Pedro Álvares Cabral. The ten suites on offer are each named after a famous Portuguese figure, and while they range in price, each guarantees a luxurious experience. The walls are adorned with original eighteenth-century azulejo tiles, there are terrific views of the surrounding terracotta rooftops from the many terraces, and guests can relax in the black marble swimming pool, shaded by overhanging orange trees.

€€€€

—

Páteo Dom Fradique 14, 1100-624 Lisboa
palaciobelmonte.com
+351 218 816 600

Palácio Ramalhete

Situated a little off the beaten track, opposite the
National Museum of Ancient Art in the lively Janelas
Verdes neighbourhood, the Palácio Ramalhete is an
attractive eighteenth-century townhouse with warm
and welcoming staff who give this former private
residence a real feeling of a home. The hotel is
adorned with beautiful yellow and blue tiles and three
courtyards full of flowers, and all of the bedrooms
have their own distinctive aesthetic and character.
Guests can take advantage of the cosy bar (where
you can choose from a small number of Portuguese
dishes) and enjoy the heated outdoor pool.

€€

—

Rua das Janelas Verdes 92, 1200-692 Lisboa
palacio-ramalhete.com
+351 213 974 752

Pousada de Lisboa

€€€

This beautiful hotel is situated very centrally, off the classical Praça do Comércio, where the Royal Palace once stood, in an opulent bright yellow Pombaline building. The hotel stays true to its eighteenth-century origins – antiques, original art, high ceilings – while showcasing modern luxury in all its glory. There are ninety tasteful suites with marble-clad bathrooms and parquet floors, the most famous being the cavernous Dom Pérignon suite, once the office of the prime minister António Salazar. If you can't quite stretch to this, ask for a room facing the São Jorge Castle for the best views. After a busy day checking out the surrounding shops and cafés, you can relax in the very modern spa and pool on the third floor, and enjoy a meal in the restaurant, Lisboeta, which serves Portuguese cuisine.

—

Praça do Comércio 31-34, 1149-018 Lisboa
pousadas.pt/en/hotel/pousada-lisboa
+351 218 442 001

Santiago de Alfama

Situated in a fifteenth-century building in the quarter surrounding the
castle, this sweet boutique hotel comprises nineteen spacious suites and
bedrooms, each with its own style, determined by the irregular dimensions
of the building. The architect Luís Rebelo de Andrade spent six years
lovingly transforming this ancient edifice into a clean and modern five-star
hotel while maintaining many of the authentic features. The fascinating
architecture of the building – some of the Roman remains are still visible
– combined with the attentive and friendly staff, make this hotel a truly
enjoyable holiday experience. Indulge in a manicure in the beauty bar;
try the ceviche or the grilled octopus in A Fábrica de Santiago, the hotel
restaurant with an international menu, and engage in some people-watching
in the hotel's Audrey Café, which spills out onto the cobbled street.

€€€

—

Rua de Santiago 10 -14, 1100-494 Lisboa
santiagodealfama.com
+351 21 394 1616

Valverde Hotel

Ideally located on Lisbon's central artery, the tree-lined Avenida da Liberdade, the Valverde Hotel was designed by acclaimed Portuguese architecture and interiors company Bastir. Comprising twenty-five comfortable bedrooms, the hotel includes two suites featuring large bathrooms with stand-alone cast-iron tubs and great views over Lisbon. Every room, however, has its own character, with opulent fabrics, 1950s furniture and some with a balcony overlooking the leafy internal courtyard. At the back of the hotel, the serene pool is beautifully decorated, with subtle corrugated iron walls. The relaxed Sítio restaurant includes a number of classic Portuguese dishes, and after dinner you can enjoy a cocktail and some fado on the patio.

€€€

—

Avenida da Liberdade 164, 1250-146 Lisboa
valverdehotel.com
+351 210 940 301

Shops

39a Concept Store

Innovative commercial space 39a, the brainchild of Raquel Prates, is a concept store in the truest sense. A combination gallery and fashion store, Prates approaches stock selection and display like a contemporary curator, and the pieces here, comprising womenswear, shoes and accessories, are displayed like works of art. That is not to say that this is a cold, intimidating experience; in fact the opposite is true. This method means that the merchandise is constantly changing and the layout of the store evolves in response. One eye-catching feature is the mural on the exposed wall that is regularly renewed by different artists, reflecting the fact that no two trips to 39a are the same.

—

Rua Alexandre Herculano 39A, 1250-009 Lisboa
39a.pt
+351 21 605 8302

Bertrand

Having opened its doors in 1732, the Chiado Bertrand Bookstore is the oldest bookstore in the world that has been in continuous use, and it is adored by Lisbon locals. After the original store was destroyed in the earthquake of 1755, the bookshop moved to its current location on Rua Garrett. It has since grown into a large and modern chain of bookshops, but the Chiado branch maintains much of its old-school charm. There is a wide selection of English-language books if Portuguese is not your thing. When you make a purchase, ask a staff member to mark it with a stamp to say that you bought the book in the world's longest-running bookstore.

—

Rua Garrett 73, 1200-309 Lisboa
bertrand.pt
+351 21 347 6122

Embaixada LX

Embaixada is the Portuguese word for embassy, and this shopping gallery, situated in the plush nineteenth-century Ribeiro da Cunha Palace in the Príncipe Real neighbourhood, certainly has the grandeur befitting the name. It is home to many small independent boutiques, with a focus on Portuguese cuisine, design and craftsmanship, and it is difficult to beat for high-end clothing and gifts. Even if you're not in the mood for shopping, call in for a drink or a bite to eat on the ground floor, and to enjoy the Moorish flourishes in the architecture.

—

Praça do Príncipe Real 26, 1250 Lisboa
embaixadalx.pt
+351 965 309 154

Fashion Clinic

Fashion Clinic is comprised of two stores, one for male clothing and one for female, both located on the fashionable Avenue Liberdade (the shop for women is in the Tivoli Forum). The stores, which are getting a new look in 2017, contain a very well-edited selection of high-end designers such as Stella McCartney, Christian Louboutin, Kenzo, Ralph Lauren, Dolce & Gabbana, Gucci and Prada, and the spaces themselves could not be more fresh and inviting. There is also a large selection of gifts and accessories.

—

Avenue Liberdade, 192-A, 1250-146 Lisboa; Avenue da Liberdade, Tivoli Forum 5, 1250-146 Lisboa
fashionclinic.com
+351 21 354 90 40

Figaro's Barbershop

Figaro's is a men-only barbershop, specialising in classic cuts from the 1920s to 1950s, including the low-faded slickback and the flat-top boogie. It was opened with the intention of bringing a taste of American barbershop culture to Lisbon. All in all, it's a highly stylised concept where every detail has been given real thought, from the vintage uniforms, to the retro décor, to the fictional hipster personas assumed by the barbers on their social media platforms. At Figaro's, the haircut and the shave are only part of the experience.

—

Rua do Alecrim 39, 1200-014 Lisboa
figaroslisboa.com
+351 21 347 0199

Ler Devagar

Located in the Alcântara district, LXFactory is a real destination point for Lisbon locals. It is a vast industrial building that has been completely transformed into an exciting creative hub that combines art, design and food, and the jewel in its crown is Ler Devagar. This impressive bookshop is widely considered to be one of the most beautiful in the world, with a huge number of books stacked wall to wall over a number of floors, and a grand staircase as the centrepiece. The bookshop has a broad cultural programme and frequently hosts concerts and events.

—

Rua Rodrigues de Faria 103, 1300 Lisboa
lerdevagar.com
+351 21 325 9992

Gelados Santini

Santini ice cream has developed quite the reputation since its first shop opened in 1949, with hordes of zealous fans claiming that it is the best in the world. You will easily identify the newly opened store in the Chiado district by the long queue, snaking outside the door. We recommend the chocolate ice cream, but suggest you order more than one flavour or you'll be tempted to rejoin the end of the queue straightaway.

—

Rua do Carmo 9, 1200-093 Lisboa
santini.pt
+351 21 346 8431

Storytailors

While you're in the Chiado area, check out Storytailors, a stunning upmarket fashion atelier set up by a duo of designers, João Branco and Luis Sanchez, in 2006. Every year the pair create a collection inspired by a fairy tale or myth. The pieces from each season's collection are made to measure on request, and are known for their creativity and originality. With a focus on tailoring, Storytailors is particularly renowned for great corsets and bustiers.

—

Calçada Ferragial 8, 1200-182 Lisboa
storytailors.pt
+351 21 343 2306

Under the Cover

In a chic and contemporary space next to the Gulbenkian Foundation, Under the Cover is a mecca for magazine buffs and design enthusiasts. This small shop offers a carefully curated selection of international magazines on a wide range of topics including fashion, food, travel, and photography. They have a particularly strong list of independent publications that can be difficult to find elsewhere, but every magazine on the shop's shelves has something special to inspire the reader.

—

Rua Marquês Sá da Bandeira 88B, 1050-060 Lisboa
underthecover.pt
+351 915 374 707

A Vida Portuguesa

Located in Chiado, A Vida Portuguesa is a treasure trove of beautiful local craft items, ranging from stationery, to toiletries, to vinegars and olive oils, to handmade rugs. Many of the products on sale here have been manufactured in Portugal for generations. With the wide range of quality products, this shop is one of the best places for souvenirs and gifts to bring home. Check out the selection of soaps in beautiful wrapping paper.

—

Rua Anchieta 11, 1200-023 Lisboa
avidaportuguesa.com
+351 21 346 5073

What
to See

Bairro Alto

Meaning 'High Quarter', Bairro Alto is one of the
five districts that make up the heart of the old city.
Traditionally a hub for writers, artists and their fellow
bohemians, it has retained its creative spirit over the
centuries, and today it is the centre of Lisbon's fantastic
nightlife. The colourful area is made up of long tight rows
of buildings that are three to four storeys high, and the
narrow, cobbled streets below are filled with cafés and
bars of all different sizes and styles. As the area comes
alive in the evenings, fado can be heard from many of
the establishments, and as the night wears on, the fun
usually begins to spill onto the street.

Baixa

Downtown Lisbon, known as Baixa, is the main shopping area of the city and has been for centuries, as evidenced in the streets named for the vendors of the past. Today, the shops are more high-end, but this is still the heart of Lisbon. The district was completely rebuilt after the earthquake of 1755, and it is Europe's earliest example of urban planning. Hours can be spent exploring the network of cobbled pedestrian streets diffusing from the Avenida da Liberdade and the many picturesque squares between, replete with pavement bars and cafés. Highlights include the Santa Justa Elevator in Rossio Square, Praça do Comércio, and the church of San Domingo, but it's enough to just meander, as there are surprises around every corner.

—

Belém

Belém is a hugely significant part of Lisbon; it was from here that some of Portugal's – and history's – greatest explorers set sail, including Magellan and Vasco da Gama. In modern-day Belém, the influence of discovery and new cultures is visible everywhere. The elaborate architecture of Belém Tower and Jerónimos Monastery is dripping with Indian, African, Asian and South American motifs, and the majestic 'Padrão dos Descobrimentos' (Monument to the Discoveries) is a tribute to all those sailors who looked back towards Lisbon as they set off to unknown lands. This is also the museum district, and home to one of the city's most famous (and calorific) treasures, the delicious Pastéis de Belém (see pg. 83). If you're planning to spend a day here, avoid Mondays, as many of the attractions are closed.

—

Castelo de São Jorge

Many of the best views in Lisbon include the São Jorge Castle, but the fortification itself, situated on the city's highest hill, also offers spectacular panoramic views of the town and river, particularly at sunset. As a destination it offers a great deal; it is steeped in history and more than worthy of the steep climb (or you can rent a tuk-tuk). Built by the Romans in the sixth century, and later inhabited by the Moors, it was conquered and claimed for the Christians by Portugal's first king, D. Afonso Henriques, in 1147. Today, you can join a free tour or go it alone to explore the castle towers and museum, and then relax in the gardens amidst the peacocks and geese.

—

R. de Santa Cruz do Castelo, 1100-129 Lisboa
castelodesaojorge.pt
+351 218 800 620

Jerónimos Monastery

Completed in 1601, Jerónimos Monastery is a UNESCO World
Heritage site and the most visually arresting monument to
Portugal's significance in the Age of Discovery. Its construction
was begun in 1501 under the direction of King Manuel I, and it was
inhabited by the Hieronymite Order, whose role was to pray for
the King's soul and to offer spiritual guidance to seafarers before
their voyages. Its ties to the tradition of exploration are visible
everywhere in its design, with its myriad ethnic and maritime
symbols, and in addition, the tomb of Vasco da Gama is inside the
entrance. To appreciate the monastery's glory at a relaxed pace,
it is best to go early in the morning or later in the day to avoid the
biggest crowds. Closed on Mondays.

—

Praça do Império, 1400-206 Lisboa
mosteirojeronimos.pt
+351 213 620 034

Museu Coleção Berardo

Museu Coleção Berardo is a museum of contemporary art situated in Belèm. The airy, spacious, and minimalist gallery displays José Berardo's collection of abstract, surrealist and pop art, including the works of David Hockney, Andy Warhol, Francis Bacon and Jackson Pollock. The temporary exhibitions are also among some of the most exciting in the country. The air-conditioned building is perfect for escaping the heat of the summertime for a few hours to indulge your inner culture vulture. There is a café looking out onto a grassy lawn, a bookshop and a craft museum store for you to enjoy while you're there. Admission is free.

—

Praça do Império, 1449-003 Lisboa
museuberardo.pt
+351 21 361 2878

Praça do Comércio

The main shopping streets of the Baixa area run down to this large plaza which looks on to the Tagus River, creating an airy and elegant open space in central Lisbon. It is often referred to as Terreiro do Paço (Terrace of the Palace) because it had been the location of the Royal Ribeira Palace before the 1755 earthquake. In the wake of that catastrophic event, the Praça do Comércio was the focus of the reconstruction carried out by the 1st Marquis of Pombal. Highlights of the square include the magnificent statue of King José I, positioned in the centre, the Arco da Rua Augusta, which marks the entrance to Rua Augusta, and the Cais das Colunas, a set of marble stairs on the southern side, which leads down to the water's edge.

—

Rossio
Square

Rossio Square, also known as Praça Dom
Pedro IV, feels like the core point of the
city centre, located as it is in the Baixa
district, and indeed it has witnessed many
important events in the city's history, from
protests to bullfights. The busy square is
lined with shops and cafés with elegant
façades, and is thus the place to come for
a lazy coffee and some people-watching.
Café Nicola (see pg. 81) is probably the
most famous spot to enjoy a drink. There
are two large baroque fountains and a
central monument, the column of Pedro IV,
which dates from 1870. The square's most
impressive building is the neoclassical
Dona Maria II National Theatre.

—

Restau-
rants

A Cevicheria

This little joint will catch your eye as you walk through the
Príncipe Real neighbourhood. The exterior looks great, and inside
it's even cooler, especially the huge octopus suspended from
the ceiling. As the name would suggest, the traditional Peruvian
seafood dish of ceviche is front and centre on the menu, with
four deliciously fresh and authentic variations to choose from.
For those not brave enough to try the ceviche, the restaurant also
offers many other South American classics, such as tacos and
empanadas. Along with the innovative menu, the clean minimal
interiors and relaxed atmosphere make this a very popular
spot. There is a no-reservation policy, but cocktails are served
onto the street through a window, so come early and sip on a
speciality Pisco Sour as you wait.

€

—

Rua D. Pedro V 129, 1200-093 Lisboa
facebook.com/ACevicheriaChefKiko
+351 21 803 8815

Bairro do Avillez

The name José Avillez is one you are very likely to come across in your travels in Lisbon. The chef has opened a number of successful restaurants around the city, and this spacious incarnation in the Chiado neighbourhood is no exception. Bairro do Avillez comprises different eating areas where you can sample the best in seafood and charcuterie, all prepared with Avillez's innovative flair. It also boasts the Mercearia, a shop where you can stock up on cheese, cured meats, gifts and books. The Taberna's range of sandwiches, soups and small dishes make it a perfect place for a pit-stop lunch, while the Páteo's fare invites a more leisurely dining experience.

€€€€

—

Rua Nova da Trindade 18, 1200-303 Lisboa
bairrodoavillez.pt
+351 215 830 290

Belcanto

Another example of José Avillez's establishments, Belcanto is currently the only restaurant in Lisbon to hold two Michelin stars. The restaurant opened in 1958 in Lisbon's historical centre of Chiado, and Avillez took the helm in 2012. With the adventurous and witty menu, the talent and perfectionism of this dynamic chef is allowed to shine; think meals entitled 'Skate Jackson Pollock' and 'The Garden of the Goose that Laid the Golden Egg'. Artistic flair is matched in the interiors, with the work of Portuguese artists adorning the walls. Diners can choose from the á la carte menu, or a tasting menu of twelve 'moments', but either way, eating here is an overwhelming gastronomic experience, where each plate is a visual spectacle as well as a culinary adventure. With a price tag you would expect from a restaurant of this calibre and only ten tables, reservations are essential.

€€€€

—

Largo de São Carlos 10, 1200-410 Lisboa
belcanto.pt
+351 213 420 607

Bico do Sapato

Part-owned by John Malkovich and Catherine Deneuve, Bico do Sapato is
one of Lisbon's chicest hotspots. It is situated in an old port building by Cais
da Pedra, with beautiful views of the water through the elegant glass walls
and from the terrace. It is a daring concept restaurant, with three different
spaces offering contrasting dining styles: for a relaxed experience you
can try the open and casual cafeteria; upstairs, there is a sushi bar serving
excellent sashimi and tempura, and the lower floor is home to a more
formal restaurant with an international menu that has a Portuguese flair
and a focus on seafood. The décor throughout is airy and sophisticated;
modern with a hint of mid-century modernism. An excellent choice for
dinner before dancing in Malkovich's neighbouring club Lux Frágil (pg. 106),
keep your eyes peeled for Lisbon's VIPs.

€€€

—

Avenida Infante D. Henrique, Armazém B, Cais da Pedra a Sta Apolónia, 1950-376 Lisboa
bicodosapato.com
+351 218 810 320

Bistro 100 Maneiras

Bistro 100 Maneiras, set in a beautiful art deco building, provides diners with a buzzing atmosphere and a fun aesthetic, the highlight of which is perhaps the dramatic portrait of chef Ljubomir Stanisic holding a pig's head. Set over two floors, with a bar and a private dining room, the restaurant's contemporary cuisine takes inspiration from Portuguese, French and Balkan cooking. If you're feeling adventurous, try some of the offerings on the 'for the brave' section of the menu (think sweetbreads and entrails). With great wine and cocktails, its doors are open and the music keeps playing until 2am, so it's perfect for night owls on their way to or from the neighbouring Bairro Alto.

€€€€

—

Largo da Trindade 9, 1200-466 Lisboa
restaurante100maneiras.com
+351 910 307 575

Clube de Jornalistas

Clube de Jornalistas opened as a press club in 1983, and there is still a boardroom in the back of the building where journalists meet. The restaurant, however, is open to all and has grown in popularity over the years, owing to the full-flavour Mediterranean food, diverse wine list, the eighteenth-century building, and the fantastic outdoor eating area. Located in the Lapa area, Restaurante Clube de Jornalistas is best experienced in the evening, so after a busy day exploring, call ahead for a table and hop onto the 28 Tram, which will leave you nearby. Try the delicious 'risotto de moqueca'.

€€

—

Rua Trinas 129, 1200-857 Lisboa
restauranteclubedejornalistas.com
+351 21 397 7138

The Decadente

The Decadente, in the Bairro Alto area, is located beneath the Independente Hostel (pg. 17). With a touch of industrial chic, this is a great casual spot to enjoy lunch and a cocktail, and the shady back patio is perfect for escaping the heat. The restaurant serves the best of modern Portuguese food, and it takes pride in the fact that the ingredients are strictly seasonal and local, where possible. For food of this quality the prices are remarkably reasonable (there is a three-course lunch menu for €10), so it's not surprising that it's extremely popular with locals, as well as tourists. Booking is recommended.

€

—

Rua de São Pedro de Alcântara 81, 1250-238 Lisboa
thedecadente.pt
+351 21 346 1381

The Insólito

They certainly got the interiors right with the Insólito, the second bar and restaurant of the Independente Hostel; there's a quirky bohemian charm to the space, with a giant bemonocled deer's head peering down on the diners, and chandeliers hanging over the chefs' heads. The real selling point of the Insólito, however, is the view. Old creaky elevators bring you to the top floor of the hostel, which feels somewhat like an attic; from here the restaurant opens out onto a rooftop terrace where the city spreads out in all its glory beneath you. Enjoy the fusion menu and the great wine and cocktail list.

€€€

—

Rua de São Pedro de Alcántara 83, 1250-238 Lisboa
theinsolito.pt
+351 21 130 3306

Mini Bar

Chiado's Mini Bar is the younger sister of the high-end Bel
Canto (see pg. 62), part of José Avillez's ever-growing empire
of restaurants, and a chance to experience the handiwork
of the Michelin-starred chef without blowing your budget.
Located in the São Luiz Theatre, Mini Bar serves evenings
only, and takes inspiration from the theatrical setting, with
red velvet curtains and a menu organised into a number of
'acts'. There is also the option of a tasting menu for the very
reasonable price of €48. The food is typical of Avillez in that
it is avant-garde, playful, and has an international flair; try the
apple and chilli-infused margarita (for eating not drinking),
the pimped-up burgers, or the foie gras Ferrero Rocher. DJ's
perform on Friday and Saturday nights, from 11pm till 2am.

€€€

—

Rua António Maria Cardoso 58, 1200-027 Lisboa
minibar.pt
+351 21 130 5393

Pharmacia

€€€

The quirky Pharmacia is housed in Lisbon's Museum of Health and Pharmacy. As the name would suggest, the interiors are inspired by vintage pharmacies, and there is an abundance of references to the theme: old medicine cabinets filled with bottles and jars, red cross logos, food served in test tubes, and waiting staff sporting white lab coats. Tasty and fresh 'Petiscos', or Portuguese tapas, are on the menu, along with cocktails, wines and light snacks from the bar. Enjoy an 'LSD' cocktail on the fantastic outside terrace.

—

Rua Marechal Saldanha 1, 1200-012 Lisboa
facebook.com/restaurantepharmacia
+351 21 346 2146

Taberna da Rua das Flores

This tiny gem in Chiado is generally full to the brim and doesn't take bookings, so be prepared to queue. The chef's reputation is what brings the crowds to this little tavern, and the simple, locally sourced food is worth the wait. The menu changes daily and is brought to your table on a large blackboard, adding to the cosy, old-fashioned vibe – speaking of which, it's cash only. The ubiquitous codfish, clams, mussels and pork shoulder are typical of the Portuguese standards available, but there is nothing standard about the flavours. The wines are all sourced from the Lisbon area, and some of their gourmet products can be purchased to bring home.

€€

—

Rua das Flores 103, 1200-194 Lisboa
+351 21 347 9418

Tabik Restaurant

Situated in the beautiful Bessa Hotel, Tabik is
an airy and modern space with massive prints
of Velázquez and Caravaggio paintings hanging
from the walls. This place is casual and as hip as it
gets, but the young chef at the helm, Manuel Lino,
takes his food very seriously and is fast making
a name for himself as a result. The daring and
delicious menu is broadly Mediterranean, with
a focus on Portuguese cooking and ingredients;
expect innovative delights such as beef tartare with
coconut foam and chili. In addition, the cocktails
are just as exciting as the food.

€

—

Avenida da Liberdade 29A, 1250-139 Lisboa
tabikrestaurant.com
+351 213 470 549

Tágide Wine & Tapas

Sister to the more formal Tágide Restaurant situated next door, this wine bar is small and simple, with a pared-back aesthetic and beautiful views over the river (so try to get a seat near the window). Choose from a wide selection of tapas (such as roasted chorizo, fish soup, sautéed prawns, octopus salad) or sharing plates (including cheeses with jam, sausage croquettes, roasted black pudding) accompanied by a bottle of wine from their extensive list, which boasts both Portuguese and international varieties. If you're passing in the afternoon, try the excellent-value lunch menu for €12.50, which includes a glass of wine and a custard tart.

€

—

Largo da Academia Nacional de Belas Artes 18-20, 1200-005 Lisboa
restaurantetagide.com
+351 213 404 010

Cafés

À Margem

This gleaming minimalist café bar (formerly a shipping container) was cleverly designed by João Pedro Falcão de Campos and Ricardo Vaz to ensure that its structure does nothing to interrupt the view, which is the real star of the show. À Margem is located on the bank of the Tagus River, and serves a range of sandwiches, light meals and drinks throughout the day. Open from 10am to 1am, try to time your visit in the evening to enjoy the sunset over the river. Its location does demand a bit of a walk, but it is a memorable option in the touristy area of Belém.

—

Doca do Bom Sucesso, 1400-038 Lisboa
amargem.com
+351 918 620 032

Café Royale

The eclectic Café Royale marries Portuguese, Mediterranean and Scandinavian influences, and the result is an easy, relaxed space with great music and a wholesome but creative menu. Owner Ana Faro, previously an architect, lovingly restored this once run-down building, and has imbued it with an understated elegance. The hamburger with tzatziki, poached egg and bacon is a local favourite, and there is also a good selection of seafood and vegetarian options. The drinks menu is extensive, with wines, craft beers, fresh juices and an interesting list of teas. The best seats in the house are in the hidden garden to the rear – the perfect spot to enjoy a kir royale before lunch.

Largo Rafael Bordalo Pinheiro 29 R/C, 1200-369 Lisboa
royalecafe.com
+351 21 346 9125

Fábulas

The discreet doorway to Fábulas, on one of the myriad stepped streets of the busy Chiado district, conceals a surprising and charming café. The dark interior, with its vaulted ceiling and walls of cool stone, has plenty of nooks and crannies, making it a calm place to read or work. There is also a gallery space that holds exhibitions, musical performances and cinema screenings. Fábulas offers peaceful seclusion inside and out, as the cavern-like interior opens out onto an airy central courtyard, which is shared with neighbouring establishments. The menu ranges from tapas and sandwiches to mains, where seafood is plentiful, and prices are reasonable. Expect to see people working on laptops during the day, before meeting friends here for the evening.

—

Calçada Nova de São Francisco 14, 1200-300 Lisboa
fabulas.pt
+351 21 601 8472

Galeto

Galeto opened in 1966, and little about it has been changed in the intervening decades. Behind the retro neon signage, the interior is art deco but there is a vintage Americana diner feel too, and while booths are available for parties of up to four, we recommend that you perch on a tiny swivel stool at the vast, meandering bar. They offer a very extensive menu that includes wicked comfort food, like fried club sandwiches and brioche burgers, so although perhaps not for the health-conscious, it is wildly popular with locals and with late-night revellers, who come when the bars have closed. Galeto is open until 3am, so it's great for an after-hours snack, but note that prices do increase after 10pm.

—

Avenida da República 14, 1050-191 Lisboa
+351 21 354 4444

Café Nicola

Café Nicola has been in operation since the late eighteenth century, and when it opened in this location in 1929, it soon became a favourite meeting place of politicians and the literati. Today, culture and tradition remain important, and diners can enjoy occasional performances of traditional fado singing at weekends. Often thronged with tourists, you can expect to pay a little extra for the café's fame and location on Rossio Square, but its cultural significance still warrants a visit; take a seat on the terrace at twilight to admire the elegant façade and observe the passing crowds on the square.

—

Praça Dom Pedro IV 24-25, 1200-091 Lisboa
+351 21 346 0579

Noobai Café

A chilled and genial crowd begins to gather on the three rooftop terraces of Noobai from late afternoon, and this is a highly recommended place to grab a cocktail and watch the sunset before a night out. Located in the Miradouro do Adamastor district, the overall vibe is extremely relaxed; come as you are, enjoy the music, and gaze out over the Tagus River. The menu is well suited to vegetarians, the health-conscious, and those with a sweet tooth. Noobai is also a popular brunch destination, and there are often DJ sets on Sundays. Closed on Monday.

—

Miradouro de Santa Catarina, 1200-401 Lisboa
noobaicafe.com
+351 21 346 5014

Pastéis de Belém

Casa Pastéis De Belém is the home of the traditional pastel de nata, the iconic little Portuguese pastries that are filled with custard and sprinkled with cinnamon. A product of the 1820 liberal revolution, which saw the neighbouring monastery closed and its inhabitants baking to secure an income, the Pastéis de Belém here are still made to the monastery's original 'secret recipe'. Stop in on your way to see Belém; the pastries are available to take away, or you can take a seat in the adjoining café, which is surprisingly large and always bustling. Be prepared to queue, but trying one of the original and best Lisbon pastries is an absolute necessity.

—

R. Belém 84-92, 1300-085 Lisboa
pasteisdebelem.pt
+351 21 363 7423

Pastelaria
Versailles

Opened in 1922, Versailles is a fitting name for this opulent art nouveau tea room, which is nothing short of a Lisbon institution. There is seating on the terrace, but try to get a spot inside to experience the bustle and old-world charm, where little has changed in almost one hundred years. The décor is exquisite, with high ceilings, luxe chandeliers and black-and-white marble floors, and the service is exemplary. A full menu is available, but we recommend breakfast, or coffee and a fresh pastry. Initially a haunt of ladies who lunch, it maintains a dedicated local clientele and is a memorable way to get a flavour of traditional Lisbon.

—

Avenida da República 15A, 1050-185 Lisboa
+351 21 354 6340

Miradouro de São Pedro

This unassuming little kiosk café is perfectly situated in a hilltop garden at one of Lisbon's most magnificent viewing points (and right in front of the Independente, pg. 17). The kiosk, which serves drinks and snacks, opened in 2010 to cater for the many tourists who come to admire the spectacular panoramic view, which takes in the city centre and the castle. If you're feeling energetic, you can hike up the Calçada da Glória to the kiosk, but otherwise you can ride the Ascensor da Glória funicular. There is often live music, so relax on a deckchair with a caipirinha or martini and enjoy the vista. A romantic way to wind down into evening. Open late on Friday and Saturday.

—

R. São Pedro de Alcântara, 1200-470 Lisboa

Sol e Pesca

Simultaneously unconventional and utterly authentic, Sol e Pesca is a quirky bar in the premises of a former fishing-equipment shop, which now serves drinks and an abundance of fresh and tinned fish, served with bread. The interior, honouring the previous tenants and the city's wider maritime culture, is fascinating, with fishing paraphernalia and cabinets bursting with the wonderfully designed colourful seafood tins. Located in Cais do Sodré, which was previously the red-light district but is now a buzzing area for nightlife, the bar is open late (until 4am at the weekend) and the courtyard teems with revellers when the nearby bars close their doors. A fun afternoon pit stop or night-time base.

—

R. Nova do Carvalho 44, 1200 Lisboa
solepesca.com
+351 21 346 7203

Bars

A Ginjinha Espinheira

This tiny hole-in-the-wall in Rossio Square was established in 1840, when the owner, Espinheira, a Galician immigrant, first served Ginja, a sweet cherry liqueur that was to become a national favourite. Today, the Ginjinha continues to sell just this drink, and has a marble vat that holds 800 litres. It is served straight in white plastic cups, with boozy cherries or without, and shots cost a mere €1.40. Sweet and potent, a quick Ginja is the perfect way to kick-start an afternoon's exploring, or as a digestif in the evening. Queues are likely but move swiftly. Fast, cheap and authentic, this is a unique experience that you won't find anywhere else.

—

1 Praça Dom Pedro IV 71, 1100-026 Lisboa

CINCO lounge

Located on a quiet street in Príncipe Real, CINCO's modest exterior (keep your eyes peeled for the candles on the steps) conceals a super chic but relaxed bar that serves some of the best cocktails in Lisbon. The interior is dark and brooding but extremely comfortable, and the music is played at a level that allows you to carry on a conversation. The service is particularly warm and knowledgeable, so allow the bartender to recommend something from their extensive list of classic and seasonal cocktails. Ranging from €7.50 to €30+, these are creative and witty concepts, with exquisite presentation, and meats and cheeses are also available if you're peckish. A smart and grown-up nightspot.

—

R. Ruben A. Leitão 17A, 1200-392 Lisboa
cincolounge.com
+351 914 668 242

O Bom
O Mau
e O Vilão

O Bom O Mau e O Vilão was named after the Clint Eastwood classic *The Good, The Bad and The Ugly*, and cinema's influence permeates this laid-back cocktail bar. It's spacious, stylish, and just the right side of retro, and alongside a strong daily offering of live music and DJ sets, film screenings are common. The space is divided into a number of rooms, each with a distinct personality, which lends the bar the feeling of a great house party. Situated in the lively Cais do Sodré district, it is open from 7pm to 2am, and to 3am on Friday and Saturday. Check their Facebook page for up-to-date listings.

—

Rua do Alecrim 21, 1200-014 Lisboa
pt.thegoodthebadandtheuglybar.com
+351 964 531 423

O Purista – Barbiere

Initially conceived as a pop-up, O Purista – Barbiere is a confident concept: a barbershop and bar in one. You can have your beard trimmed as you enjoy one of their excellent gin and tonics, then have a beer and play pool to the backdrop of live music or DJ sets at the weekend. The space used to house a bookshop, and the aesthetic is vintage but not dusty, with cool black-and-white tiles, lots of exposed lightbulbs, and a backlit wall of beer bottles. The staff are particularly friendly and efficient, and the overall atmosphere is amiable and chilled. This is the manliest bar in town, but it's extremely popular with both sexes.

—

Rua Nova da Trindade 16C, 1200 302 Lisboa
+351 968 614 566

Park bar

Park Bar is situated on the roof of the EMEL multistorey car park in Bairro Alto. Take the car-park lift to the sixth floor and walk the final flight of steps, which opens out onto a garden terrace with amazing 180-degree views over the city, including the Santa Catarina church and the 25 de Abril Bridge. The spectacular view is contrasted with low-key furniture and lots of lush foliage, and the result is effortlessly cool. Come for a lunchtime burger and watch twilight fall with a cocktail or sangria, as the house DJ raises the tempo into the early hours.

—

Calçada do Combro 58, 1200-115 Lisboa
+351 21 591 4011

Pavilhão Chinês

The weathered exterior of Pavilhão Chinês hints
at the history but not the opulence or scale of this
Lisbon institution. Ring the doorbell to enter this
treasure trove, which offers an experience as close
to cocktail hour in a museum as you're likely to get.
The building used to house a grocery store, and
now its myriad cabinets are bursting with quirky
vintage artefacts – from toy soldiers to Christmas
baubles – and almost every surface displays
interesting antiques. Staff in old-school uniforms
survey the bar's five refined and cosy rooms, and
serve superior cocktails from an exhaustive menu.

—

Rua Dom Pedro V 89, 1250-093 Lisboa
facebook.com/pavilhaochineslisboa
+351 21 342 4729

Pensão Amor

The eighteenth-century premises of Pensão Amor ('The Guesthouse of Love') was formerly a brothel, and the new occupants have embraced its colourful history with aplomb. There are two entrances: the front way leads straight to the main parlour, with its lush fabrics, chandeliers and artworks of female and male nudes; the other leads from the pink Rua Nova do Carvalho and introduces the lavish but anarchic interior with sexy graffiti adorning the walls. The bar occupies three floors and there is lots to explore, including kissing booths, a pole-dancing room, and a room lined with fur. Although the setting is wild, the clientele is relaxed and fun, and this is a very popular hangout with artists and musicians. Prices go up €1 after 10pm, so get there earlier to choose the best seat and watch the crowd grow.

—

Rua do Alecrim 19, 1200-292 Lisboa
pensaoamor.pt
+351 21 314 3399

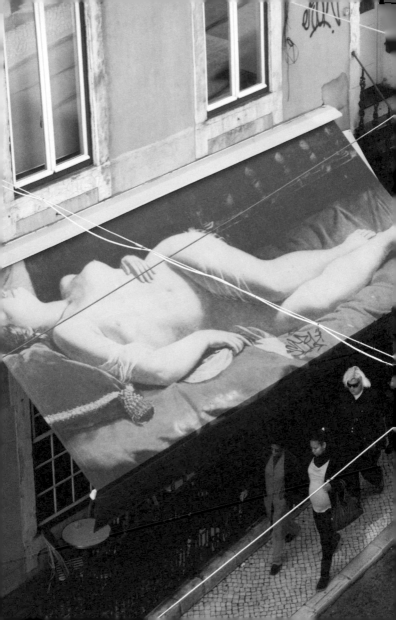

Tivoli Sky Bar

Lisbon is spoiled with great rooftop bars, and the stunning Sky Bar, atop the five-star Tivoli Hotel, is one of its most luxurious. Previously a seasonal feature, as of 2017 the Sky Bar is open year round, and it is a chic space from which to enjoy the magnificent ninth-floor views. The white furniture and floor cushions, combined with a clever lighting system and fabulous illuminated bar, imbue the Sky Bar with a soft glow and warm atmosphere. The crowd is chilled but well-heeled, and you can expect to pay a little more for this location. Cocktails are €10 and the food menu, offering tapas, salads and burgers, ranges from €7 to €17. House DJs and live bands provide the soundtrack on Thursdays, Fridays and Saturdays.

—

Av. da Liberdade 185, 1269-050 Lisboa
tivolihotels.com
+351 21 319 8832

TOPO

TOPO is perched on the sixth and top floor of the Martim Moniz mall In a multicultural part of town that is growing in popularity. The interior is stripped-back cool, with ceiling-high windows to make the most of the view, and the terrace, with its stepped wooden platforms, looks right out to the São Jorge Castle. The signature cocktail menu was designed by the minds behind CINCO (see pg. 91), and the food menu is more adventurous that some of its contemporaries', with dishes like gyoza, veal tartare, and octopus fried rice featuring alongside the usual burgers and croquettes. Hunt out TOPO before sunset to secure your seat to admire the sensational skyline. Closed on Mondays.

—

6th floor, Commercial Center Martim Moniz, Praça Martim Moniz, 1100-341 Lisboa
topo-lisboa.pt
+351 21 588 1322

Clubs

B.Leza

B.Leza is a genuinely unique place to spend
a fun night of frenetic, sweaty dancing. It was
established in 1995 and relocated to this riverside
warehouse in 2012. It specialises in African and
Latin American music: performers from around
Africa and Brazil play irresistible rhythmic music
and the dancefloor throngs with upbeat patrons.
Open Wednesday to Sunday, from 10.30pm to
4am, its programme also includes accessible
dance classes, fado events and poetry readings.
Check its Facebook page for listings. An
energising place to let your hair down.

—

Rua da Cintura do Porto de Lisboa, armazém B, Cais da Ribeira Nova, 1200-109 Lisboa
+351 21 010 6837

Lust in Rio

Lust in Rio is a hugely popular open-air bar and club that is centrally located, close to the Cais do Sodré train station. It operates during the summer months, beginning at midnight and staying open very late, commonly until 6am. The late opening and great music attracts big crowds, but the main draw is the outdoor area, with views over the Tagus River. Lust in Rio regularly hosts guest DJs and performers, but a high-octane crowd is all but guaranteed every night. With its great location, good music, and open-air space for the hot Lisbon evenings, Lust in Rio is the place to go for a night out that is sophisticated and bursting with summer energy.

—

Rua Da Cintura do Porto de Lisboa 255, 1200-109 Lisboa
facebook.com/LustLisbon
+351 918 788 868

Lux Frágil

Lux Frágil is a flagship Lisbon superclub set over three levels of a huge warehouse on the docks. Part-owned by John Malkovich, its interior is suitably theatrical, and there is a great roof terrace where you can watch the sunrise as the night winds down. Entry is more competitive as the evening wears on, so get there before the bars close to have the best chance. Note that the door policy is somewhat unpredictable; you should expect to pay a €10-30 entrance fee. Music varies, so check the website for listings to ensure you hit Lux on the right night. Open Tuesday to Saturday, 11pm to 6am.

—

Av. Infante D. Henrique, Armazém A,
Cais da Pedra a Sta Apolónia, 1950-376 Lisboa
luxfragil.com
+351 21 882 0890

Musicbox

Musicbox opened in 2006 and quickly
established itself as one of the city's most
popular clubs. It's located in a nineteenth-
century warehouse under an aqueduct in 'Pink
Street', in lively Cais do Sodré, and crowds
flock here as the neighbouring bars close (it
is open Tuesday to Saturday, 11pm to 5am).
The venue prides itself on eclectic music and
independent programming, mixing club nights
with live performances and frequently playing
host to top Portuguese and international bands
and DJs. Entry generally ranges from €8 to €14.

—

Rua Nova do Carvalho, 24 1249-002 Lisboa
musicboxlisboa.com
+351 213 473 188

Silk

Silk is a nightclub, bar and Japanese restaurant with the most amazing panoramic views of the city from its large open-air terrace. Centrally located on the sixth floor of the commercial building Espaço Chiado, the atmosphere of the club is sexy, exclusive and sophisticated. Before you take the elevator up to enjoy the view, email them and check availability for the evening, as they pride themselves on their stringent entry policy.

—

Rua da Misericórdia 14, 1200-273 Lisboa
silk-club.com
+351 913 009193

Markets

Feira da Ladra

The Feira da Ladra (or 'Thieves' Market') is held on Tuesdays and Saturdays, and the extent of its colourful merchandise has to be seen to be believed. The second-hand wares are of varied quality, but interesting knickknacks, collectables and antiques are to be found on the stalls and stretched out on blankets. There has been a market at this location for over three hundred years, and while today all the trading is above board, pickpockets still operate here, so be mindful of your belongings. The market is on the Tram 28 route, so come prepared to explore for hours and, of course, be ready to haggle.

Tuesday, 6am to 2pm; Saturday, 6am to 5pm.

—

Campo de Santa Clara, 1100-472 Lisboa
+351 21 817 0800

Mercado da Ribeira

In 2014, magazine *Time Out* created the Mercado da Ribeira in the 1892 shell of a previous market and in a short space of time it has become the city's favourite meeting place. Two million visitors pass through every year to visit the dozens of restaurants and bars (not to mention shops and produce stalls) that showcase the best that the city has to offer, and allow its top chefs to sell their food for more attractive prices. The embodiment of *Time Out*'s curation process and high critical standards, inclusion is a gleaming seal of approval for local businesses, and every taste is catered for. The food is exquisite, the design is stylish and the space is always full of life, making this an unbeatable place for lunch.

Sunday to Wednesday, 10am to 12am; Thursday to Saturday, 10am to 2am.

—

Avenida 24 de Julho 49, 1200-109 Lisboa
timeoutmarket.com
+351 21 359 1274

Mercado de Campo de Ourique

The Mercado de Campo de Ourique has been the core of one of Lisbon's most traditional neighbourhoods since 1934. Refurbished in 2013, it is now an eclectic and slick urban food market and one of the most popular spots to dine, drink and people-watch. Alongside the traditional fresh food stalls there are numerous styles of cuisine on offer, with a focus on classic Portuguese products, fresh seafood and high-quality fusion cooking, all served in a stylish environment that is more intimate than the Mercado da Ribeira.

Open daily, 10am to 11pm (1am Thursday to Saturday); limited opening on Sundays.

—

Rua Coelho da Rocha, 104, 1350-075 Lisboa
facebook.com/MercadoCampoDeOurique
+351 21 396 2272

Parks

Jardim
da Estrela

Situated a stone's throw from the stunning Estrela Basilicia, this is the quintessential city park, and it is no surprise that it is popular with families. The park is wonderfully maintained, with a wide variety of trees and lush vegetation, a big playground, and a little pond that is home to ducks and turtles. Look out for the wrought-iron bandstand, and for the tiny bookshop pavilion in the centre, where you can buy books, newspapers and magazines to read at the lake-side café. A favourite with locals and visitors, this park is the perfect place to rest a while or to enjoy a family picnic.

Open daily, 7am to midnight.

—

Praça da Estrela, 1200-667 Lisboa

Parque Eduardo VII

Those who undertake to travel to this park on foot will be rewarded with one of the most spectacular views of Lisbon. The park is named for British King Edward VII who was overcome by this vista in 1902. The park itself is large (covering 26 hectares) and is more rigidly designed and manicured than its counterparts, with a large flat space in the centre bordered by tree-lined promenades, as well as a tropical hothouse and greenhouse. This is a popular sunbathing spot during high season, so if travelling to the park on foot, a morning start is advised. There is a lakeside tapas restaurant at the summit where you can unwind with lunch on the terrace.

Open daily, 7am to midnight.

—

Avenida Sidonio Pais, 1070-051 Lisboa

Jardim do Príncipe Real

The nineteenth-century Jardim do Príncipe Real (officially the Jardim França Borges) is a small but perfectly formed oasis in the affluent and bohemian Príncipe Real neighbourhood. Surrounded by a perimeter of interesting bars, shops and antique specialists, the park is lively but not crowded, offering a cool place to hang out with a coffee from one of the beautiful kiosks. There is a shaded playground for children and a market on Saturdays, but the star of the show is the incredible 140-year-old cypress tree in the centre, with its umbrella of branches reaching over 20 feet in diameter.

Open daily, 7am to midnight.

—

Praça do Príncipe Real, 1250-096 Lisboa

Check
What's
On

Brunch Electronik
Cinemateca Portuguesa
Coliseu dos Recreios
MEO Arena
D. Maria II National Theatre

Brunch Electronik

Brunch Electronik is a weekly festival that runs on Sundays throughout the spring, summer, and autumn, at venues that change depending on the season. An inclusive, family friendly event, it combines electronic music, children's entertainment and gastronomic delights. The festival hosts the best DJs from Portugal and beyond, and children are well entertained by 'Petit Brunch', which includes activities like craft workshops, face painting and bouncy castles. When all the dancing makes you want to refuel, you can choose from a range of healthy organic foods, and check out the market where emerging brands sell their goods. Have a look at their website for tickets and to see what's on during your stay.

—

lisboa.brunchelectronik.com

Cinemateca Portuguesa

Cinemateca Portuguesa opened in 1948 and as well as a cinema, it is the National Film Archive and Museum of Portugal. Housed in a beautiful nineteenth-century art nouveau building, it has small, cosy screens that show classic films in all languages. The programme is exquisitely curated, celebrating as it does Portuguese and international cinema of all eras. A visit to Cinemateca Portuguesa would not be complete without exploring its fabulous museum; divided into three rooms, it tells the story of cinema through film reels, photographs, artefacts, and interactive displays. There is also a very highly regarded restaurant and bar, a terrace and a bookshop; all the ingredients for a rewarding day of culture. A great escape for a rainy day.

—

Rua Barata Salgueiro 39, 1269-059 Lisboa
cinemateca.pt
+351 21 359 6200

Coliseu dos Recreios

Built in 1890, the Coliseu dos Recreios is a beautiful concert hall under a stunning iron domed roof, which has played host to some of the world's most influential performers, from Pavarotti to Miles Davis to Lou Reed. The hall is octagonal in plan, holds around 4,000 people and has a diverse programme of theatre, ballet, opera and circus performances. But don't be fooled by its history or traditional décor; fantastic alternative music acts often perform here – recent notable visitors include PJ Harvey, Belle and Sebastian, and Anohni. Centrally located, this is an ornate but intimate space for gigs; check the listings before you go, as the shows here are often the hottest tickets in town.

—

Rua Portas de Santo Antão 96, 1150-269 Lisboa
coliseulisboa.com
+351 21 324 0580

MEO Arena

MEO Arena is Portugal's largest indoor events venue, and this is where the world's biggest music names perform in Lisbon (recent acts include Adele, Muse and The Cure). Built in 1998, it is a slick and well-organised arena with great acoustics. It is located in the cool and contemporary Parque das Nações area by the waterfront, and you can ride a cable car from here over the Tagus River. There are lots of interesting shops, bars and restaurants nearby, so if you're going to a show, come a few hours early to look around and have dinner.

—

Rossio dos Olivais, 1990-231 Lisboa
arena.meo.pt
+351 21 891 84 09

D. Maria II National Theatre

On the north side of Rossio Square stands the Dona Maria II National Theatre, a monumental neoclassical building built in the 1840s. It is situated on the site of the former Inquisitor's Palace. The portico has six Ionic columns, and atop the pediment is a statue of playwright Gil Vicente. The theatre has two separate venues that host classical music performances and plays. The works staged here are mostly classical, by both Portuguese and international playwrights, and it is from here that the National Theatre Company operates.

—

Praça D. Pedro IV, 1100-201 Lisboa
teatro-dmaria.pt
+351 21 325 0800

Before you visit Lisbon, you might want to check out these books and films to give you a better sense of the city.

Books

An Explanation of the Birds
António Lobo Antunes

An Explanation of the Birds illuminates the struggles of Rui S., a man tormented by his bourgeois family, and, even worse, by his bigoted communist second wife Marilia. In this abusive marriage she tries to involve him in her Communist cell. During the story, which is set in the course of post-revolutionary Lisbon, Rui suffers a mental breakdown, and bit by bit creates a surreal, dreamy world in which there is no boundary between fact and fiction.

The Following Story
Cees Nooteboom

This pocket-sized little gem by the Nobel Prize candidate Cees Nooteboom is a surreal journey through memories, dreams, and meditations about the meaning of life. Hermann Mussert, a misanthropic former teacher of Greek and Latin obsessed with classical antiquity, is certainly not a typical hero. Going to bed one night in Amsterdam, and waking in the morning in a hotel room in Lisbon that was the scene of an important romantic moment in his life, he has a strange feeling that he might be dead. After a strongly metaphoric journey, the novel reveals its rather witty structure, and the reader has a chance to put together the small pieces of this unusual character.

Skylight
José Saramago

Skylight is one of the earliest works by Portuguese author José Saramago, but it was not published until sixty years after it was written in 1953, and a year after the acclaimed author's death. It starts with an epigraph from Raul Brandão: 'In all souls, as in all houses, beyond the façade lies a hidden interior', which refers to the voyeuristic nature of the book. Saramago lets us peek into a dodgy apartment building in the 1940s in the heart of Lisbon, with six flats and fifteen people, among them middle-class families, couples, a sales rep, a kept woman, and a cobbler. As we are taken through different stories and struggles in the loosely plotted narrative, the reader is the only person who never leaves the building.

The Year of the Death of Ricardo Reis
José Saramago

Written in Saramago's offbeat style, and with no

punctuation except commas and full stops, *The Year of the Death of Ricardo Reis* charts the final year in the life of the title character. The story opens with Reis, who was one of the heteronyms deployed by the poet Fernando Pessoa, receiving the news that his alter ego has died. As a result, he returns to Lisbon from Brazil, where he had emigrated, and instead of continuing his practice as a doctor, he spends his days reading and wandering the streets. From time to time Pessoa's spirit appears, and the poets discuss existential issues, and this dreamy novel is rich with references to Portuguese history.

Films

Colossal Youth
(2006)

This heavy, controversial piece reveals the darker side of Lisbon and the Portuguese spirit. Mixing documentary and fiction, this unique work is set in Lisbon's Fontainhas neighbourhood, where this seventy-five-year-old immigrant Ventura faces relocation because of a housing project. The film, with its very slow, dark cinematography, shows Ventura's visits to his 'children', and their long conversations, which are mixed with a dream-like environment to eerie effect.

Lisbon Story
(1994)

Directed by the celebrated Wim Wenders, *Lisbon Story* is a unique piece, not only for its charming, dreamy depiction of Lisbon, but because of its connections to other Wenders movies. Philip Winter, a sound engineer, comes to Lisbon to work on a film, but he arrives to discover that the director of the movie has disappeared. Although the circumstances are rather strange, he decides to continue recording the sound for the film – motivated mostly by an attractive Portuguese singer called Teresa. After watching *Lisbon Story* it is hard not to fall in love with the city.

Mysteries of Lisbon
(2010)

With its four-and-a-half hour running time, *Mysteries of Lisbon* is an epic piece of work. Based on an 1854 novel by Camilo Castelo Branco, the movie focuses on an orphan boy called João, but it comprises a series of interconnected stories. The first part deals with João's past, while the second reveals his later years, travelling in Italy and France. This mesmerising journey through the nineteenth century is a visual masterpiece, and is definitely recommended viewing before travelling to Lisbon.

Tabu
(2012)

Tabu is a slow, gentle, and intimate black-and-white drama by Miguel Gomes. Divided into two parts, first we encounter an elderly lady who is seeking a man from her past, and this is followed by the story of her life, told in flashback. While the setting of the first part resembles present-day Lisbon, that of the latter is an idyllic rural setting in Mozambique and the film reveals a lot about colonialism and the period before the Portuguese Colonial War.

Check out these sites and accounts for the most up-do-date events and insights into Lisbon life:

Influencers

Agenda Cultural de Lisboa
agendalx.pt

For the latest news and events in Lisbon.

Atlas Lisboa
atlaslisboa.com

Founded by a surfer from Memphis and a mountaineer from Belarus, Atlas Lisboa is particularly useful for outdoor types, with great recommendations for activities like surfing, biking and climbing.

Eat Drink Lisbon
eatdrinklisbon.blogspot.ie

A lovingly crafted selection of Lisbon's charming bars and eateries.

Lisboa Diarios
lisboadiarios.blogspot.ie

'The Lisbon Diary' is an evocative photography blog by Artur Lourenço that captures the colour of the city.

Lisbon Lux
lisbonlux.com

A bilingual site for further recommendations and day-trip tips.

Salt of Portugal
saltofportugal.com

A blog operated by four friends who share their top tips for Lisbon and beyond in a warm and inviting way.

Underdogs
under-dogs.net

A contemporary art collective with a focus on urban culture. Encompasses exhibitions, an art store, and public art tours.

Tips from the inside: we asked some top Lisbon creatives for their favourite spots

Contributors

Manuel Aires Mateus
airesmateus.com

Manuel Aires Mateus is a prolific Lisbon architect, and the recipient of numerous national and international awards. He runs his influential studio, Aires Mateus, with his brother Francisco.

'Lisbon is a historical city, born of its geography and its relationship with the river. Urbanistically and architecturally, the city reflects overlapping eras. Thus, I suggest a walk along the river, and to witness the progression of time, I would recommend a visit to the Portuguese Gothic–Manueline Jerónimos church (pg. 51), then the Mannerist Monastery of S. Vicente de Fora (Largo de São Vicente), and finally a visit to the contemporary Calouste Gulbenkian Foundation (gulbenkian.pt).'

José Avillez
instagram.com/joseavillez

Michelin-star chef José Avillez has six restaurants in Lisbon and another in Oporto. A regular on Portuguese television, he has also published a number of cookery books.

'Bairro do Avillez (pg. 60) is my most recent project: it consists of several restaurant concepts, and it is a place filled with delicious dishes that reflect the Lisbon experience and marry tradition with cosmopolitan style. Here you may have lunch, dinner, snacks or drinks, from noon to midnight, seven days a week. Another personal favourite of mine is Miradouro de São Pedro de Alcântara (pg. 86). Located at the top of the Glória Elevator, it offers a beautiful 180-degree view of Lisbon, both during the day and at night (when it is a popular meeting place for young people).'

Miguel Castro Silva
miguelcastrosilva.com

Miguel Castro Silva is one of the most celebrated chefs in Portugal. Credited with bringing Portuguese cooking into the twenty-first century, he operates three eateries in Lisbon.

'First of all, I would like to recommend my own places: De Castro at Praça das Flores, Less at Príncipe Real, and my place at Mercado da Ribeira Time Out (pg. 114). At De Castro I serve Portuguese comfort food, and the style at Less is freer, from fish tartare to risottos. For breakfast I recommend La Boulangerie (near Museu Nacional de Arte Antiga, museudearteantiga.pt, also worth a visit) and Choupana Caffé (Av. Da Republica).'

Lunch could be at Tasca da Esquina (in Campo de Ourique), and for dinner I might choose Alma (almalisboa.pt), but if you're feeling more experimental go to Loco from Alexandre Silva (loco.pt).'

daytime. Then there is 1º de Maio, which is another good tasca and one of the oldest restaurants in Bairro Alto. For something more special, you can't go wrong in any of José Avillez's places.'

Odeith
@odeith

Sérgio Odeith has been a graffiti artist since the 1990s. He is internationally acclaimed for his anamorphic street art, which uses texture, angles and perspective to produce 3-D effects.

'Walking around the Praça da Figueira square to the Praça do Comércio square, there are a lot of good bars – small local places where you can have traditional Portuguese food. It's great to have a beer at one of the pavement tables and observe thousands of people from different countries passing by – it's truly inspiring and captivating.'

Lucy Pepper
@lucypepper

Lisbon-based Lucy Pepper is an English artist, illustrator, animator and writer. She writes a weekly bilingual column in observador.pt.

'As well as fancier places, I always advise visiting proper tascas. These are traditional Portuguese restaurants that are basic, down to earth and genuine. I particularly like Casa Cid, which is a proper no-frills spot behind Mercado da Ribeira; Fábulas (pg. 79), a nice place serving good food, and O Vicente (Rua das Flores), which has great food and a very strong wine list. Príncipe do Calhariz is a slightly more upmarket tasca, which is good for

Studio AH—HA
studioahha.com

Studio AH—HA is a communication and graphic design studio established in 2011 by Carolina Cantante and Catarina Carreiras. Their work encompasses numerous creative fields, including interior design, brand strategy and identity, advertising, product design, and illustration.

'Once a very rough area, Intendente is the next cool part of Lisbon. We recommend you take a walk through the neighbourhood and visit A Vida Portuguesa (pg. 42), for curated high-end traditional souvenirs. At the top of Chiado, Caza das Vellas Loreto (cazavellasloreto.com.pt) is a beautiful old shop selling the best handmade candles. If you are nearby and hear a bell ring, it means that some hot pasteis de nata are fresh from the oven of Manteigaria (facebook. com/manteigariacamoes/). There are many fiea markets in Lisbon, but Feira das Almas (feiradasalmas.org) has brought a fresh concept to the city: instead of people selling old and used stuff, the focus is on up-and-coming brands and new artists showcasing their work.'

Raquel Tavares
@raqueltavaresfado

Raquel Tavares is a singer of fado, and has been performing since she was a child. A leading light in the contemporary fado movement, she has released four albums and performs regularly throughout Europe.

'Calouste Gulbenkian Foundation resembles a paradise in Lisbon's city centre, where the artworks are exhibited in two amazing museum buildings. There are also frequent dance and music events held here, most notably the jazz season every summer. The beautiful park, with its outstanding sculptures, open-air amphitheatre and refreshing lakes, is worth the visit alone.'

Joana Vasconcelos
joanavasconcelos.com

Artist Joana Vasconcelos lives and works in Lisbon. She has been exhibiting internationally since the mid-1990s, and, among other works, has adorned the Venice Biennale with tampons and installed a pink feathered helicopter in the Palace of Versailles.

'Torre de Belém is not only one of my favourite spots in Lisbon, it is a source of inspiration for my work. Located on the right bank of the Tagus River, it's a sumptuous example of the Manueline style (also known as Portuguese Late Gothic), with such rich ornamentation, composed of maritime elements and representations of the discoveries, that I like to refer to it as "the Jewel of the Tagus", which is the title I gave to the temporary installation that I created for it in 2008.'

Vhils
@vhils

Alexandre Farto is a world-renowned street artist who uses an excavation technique, carving through layers of posters and plaster to create haunting large-scale

works that have changed the face of the art form.

'The new Underdogs Art Store | Montana Lisboa (cafe.montanashoplisboa.com) in Cais do Sodré is definitely a favourite. Part store, part café, it blends these two worlds, celebrating the universe of urban art and creativity. You can find cutting-edge artworks and screen prints, books, art supplies, book a street art tour, or enjoy locally brewed artisanal beer, light meals and other delicacies while taking in the sweeping views of Lisbon harbour, just five steps away. The whole district of Cais do Sodré is a favourite of mine.'

Photography Credits

Pg.106 Lux Fragil, Luísa Ferreira, Pg.108 Music box, Alpio Padilha, Pg.109 Silk, Pg.110 Daryl Lim, Pg.112 Rita Queiroz, Pg.113 Rita Queiroz, Pg.114 Mercado da Riberia, Pg.115 Mercado da Riberia, Pg.116 Mercado de Campo, Pg.118 Musica No Espaço, Pg.120 Gubin Yury/Shutterstock.com, Pg.122 S-F/Shutterstock.com, Pg.123 Alatryste/Wikicommons, Pg.124 Brunch Electronik, Pg.126 Brunch Electronik, Pg.128 Cinemateca Portuguesa, Félix Ribeiro, Pg.129 Getty Images/Pedro Gomes/Contributor, Pg.130 dynamosquito/Wikicommons, Pg.131 Artur Bogacki/Shutterstock.com, Pg. 132 Jose Ignacio Soto/Shutterstock.com